WHAT YOU MUST KNOW ABOUT

SOCIAL SECURITY

Quick & Easy!

by: Ron Stewart

© Copyright 2016 Ronald A. Stewart
All Rights Reserved

Published by:

Ronald A. Stewart
P.O. Box 340901
Brooklyn, NY 11234-0901
Editorial Consultant: Sharleen Leahey

No part of this publication, EBook, or Audio Book may be reproduced in any form without the written permission of the copyright holder listed above.

Important Notice

This book is not intended to give legal or financial advice. It is intended to give general information only. Though every effort has been made to insure accuracy, we cannot guarantee it. Rules, regulations and procedures may change over time. Free advice is available from the Social Security Administration and readers are urged to avail themselves of it before filing for any benefits. The author, publisher, editors and distributors of this book disclaim any legal liability for any damages or monetary losses resulting from the use of the information in this publication.

TABLE OF CONTENTS

Introduction vii
Purpose of This Book... vii
Some SS Acronyms.. viii

Chapter One 1
Decisions You Will Have to Make 1
Question 1. Are You Eligible for Social Security
    Retirement Benefits?... 1
Question 2. Will You Continue to Work at Early
    Retirement Age?.. 2
Question 3. How Long Will You Live?......................... 2
Question 4. How Badly Will I Need the Money at Age 62?........ 3
Question 5. Do you Want Medicare at Age 65?........... 4
Question 6. Savings, IRAs, Other Retirement Funds, Mattress
    Money, Friends and Relatives................................. 4
Question 7. What is my Projected Expense Budget at
    Age 62? 4
Don't Just Follow Others! 5
When is Break Even?.. 5
Retire Early and Invest the Money?............................. 6
What About My Spouse? 6
"File and Suspend" is Now Suspended 7
How Much Will I Receive Monthly?............................. 7

What if I am Divorced?... 8
What if My "X" Passes Away? 9
What if I Remarry? 9
Caring for X's Children Under 16 or Disabled 10
Decisions for Widows and Widowers 10
A Strategy to Maximize Monthly Benefits 11
The Right to Appeal SSA Decisions 12

Chapter Two **13**
Social Security Disability Insurance [SSDI]............................. 13
Who is Eligible for SSDI? 14
To claim disability benefits, you must meet two
    different earnings tests: 14
Paperwork Required for Filing for SSDI Benefits..................... 16
Information and Documents Required for SSDI 16
What Happens Next? 17
If You Are Approved 18
Getting a Disability Attorney to Help You 18
Hiring A Disability Attorney 19
Disability Attorney Fees 19
Beware of Disability Attorney Expenses 20
Appealing SSDI Decisions 20
How About Benefits for My Family? 21
Medicare Health Coverage 22
ABLE and the ABLE Act... 22
Going Back to Work 22
Work-at-Home Jobs 23

Chapter Three **25**
Some Important Info About Social Security 25
Same-Sex Married Couples 25

Social Security and Working Overseas 26
Criminal Convictions, Probation or Parole 26
Create Your Own "My Social Security" Online Account 26
Benefit or No Benefit SSA Verification Letters 28
If You Need Additional Information About SS 28
Sources of Additional Information on SS: 29

Chapter Four 31
Identity Theft and Protecting Your SS Number! 31
Some Ideas to Protect Yourself 32
Protect Your Bank Checking Account 33
Seniors Are Being Targeted 34
Protect Your Relatives, Friends and Yourself! 35
Free Credit Bureau Reports 35
Free Credit Score 36

Chapter Five 37
Social Security Scams to Watch Out For 37
Scam Prevention Rules of the Road 37
The COLA Scam 39
The Data-Breach Scam 40
Digital Chip Social Security Card Scam 41
Beware of Other SS Scams and Fraud 42

Chapter Six 43
The Future of Social Security and Medicare 43
Happy 81th Anniversary! 43
Social Security Trust Funds may be Depleted in 2034 43
Some Suggested Social Security Fixes 44
Part of Medicare May Be in Trouble in Year 2028 45
"Social Security and Medicare Remain Secure in the
    Medium-Term" … 46

I hope You Liked This Book…	47
Please E-mail Me …	47
Addendum	48

INTRODUCTION

Purpose of This Book

I have purchased hundreds of books over the years but unfortunately, I never had time to read most of them. Many of the ones that I did read, I didn't finish. Those 200 to 300 page books may be very well written but the problem is that very often the information I am looking for is buried in those pages like the proverbial *"needle in the hay stack!"*

Another problem is that too many older men and women nearing retirement age are not computer literate and find it frustrating, if not impossible, to navigate the Internet.

This book is designed to help you find the important information you need on Social Security *Quick and Easy,* as the title states. Naturally, I can't give you 300 pages of information in 60 plus pages. But I can give you an easy-to-read summary of the important information that the **average single person, or married couple,** getting close to early retirement age is probably seeking. If you have complicated SS situations (such as disabled children, multiple marriages, etc.), by all means get one of the 300 page books that may cover your personal situation in greater detail. *Readers Digest* has been around since 1922 which is a good indication that many people prefer or only have time for a *"Quick and Easy"* book like this one.

Please note that rules, regulations and procedures may change. Free advice is available from the Social Security Administration and readers are urged to avail themselves of it before filing for any benefits. Phone SSA toll free at **1-800-772-1213 for free advice**

Some SS Acronyms

Below are some acronyms we will use to save space and avoid repeating the same words multiple times.

COLA – Cost of Living Adjustment. There was no COLA for 2016 as the lower cost of gasoline brought down the rate of inflation (or so they say).

ERA – Early Retirement Age. 62

FICA – Federal Insurance Contributions Act. This is the federal law which requires employers to withhold three separate taxes from the wages they pay their employees. In 2016, the Social Security Tax was 6.2% to be paid by the employer and 6.2% to be paid by the employee (total 12.4%). For Medicare, the employer pays 1.45% and the employee pays another 1.45% (total 2.9%).

In 2013, a Medicare surtax of 0.9% was added when an employee earns over $200,000 per year, paid only by the employee.

FRA – Full Retirement Age. 66 to 67 years of age for most people nearing retirement. (See SSWS)PIA – Primary Insurance Amount. The monthly benefit amount you can receive at full retirement age.

SS – Social Security

SSA – Social Security Administration

SSDI – Social Security Disability Insurance

SSI – Supplemental Security Income

SSWS – Social Security Web Site. https://www.ssa.gov/

CHAPTER ONE

Decisions You Will Have to Make

Once you reach **Early Retirement Age (62)** you will have to decide if you want to start receiving your Social Security Benefits Immediately. However, you will receive a lower monthly payment which may be reduced by $1000 (or more) per month. You have the option of either waiting until **Full Retirement Age** (approximately 67) to receive a larger amount of money as your retirement benefit each month, or to age 70 when you will qualify to receive the maximum amount.

Question 1. Are You Eligible for Social Security Retirement Benefits?

If you worked a **_minimum of 10 years_** and have accumulated **_40 credits_** with Social Security you are eligible to start receiving SS benefits at age 62. You earn one credit for each $1,130 you earned (maximum 4 credits per year), provided that both you and your employer paid FICA taxes.

Question 2. Will You Continue to Work at Early Retirement Age?

If you take early retirement benefits and continue to work, Social Security will deduct $1 from your monthly benefits for every $2 you earn over $15,720. If Social Security withholds a portion of your benefits because you earned over the limit, they will pay you a higher monthly benefit when you reach Full Retirement Age. The good news is that once you reach Full Retirement Age (66-67) you will be able to earn an unlimited amount of money without SS making any deductions.

Question 3. How Long Will You Live?

When you are considering when to collect retirement benefits, one important factor to take into account is how long you might live.

According to data compiled by the Social Security Administration:

- A man reaching age 65 today can expect to live, on average, until age 84.3.

- A woman turning age 65 today can expect to live, on average, until age 86.6.

Remember those are just averages. About one out of every four 65-year-olds today will live past age 90, and one out of 10 will live past age 95.

When Social Security first started in 1935, life expectancy for a male was 59.9 years and 63.9 for a female. This is one of the reasons why SS has such a large projected deficit. With medical science pushing the limits, no one really knows what life expectancy will be in the future. One reason you must carefully consider trying to receive your maximum retirement benefit is that you may live a lot longer than you might expect to right now!

Want to know your life expectancy? You can go online to www.socialsecurity.gov and use their simple **Life Expectancy Calculator** to get a rough estimate of how long you (or your spouse) may live. Knowing this information can help you make a more informed choice regarding when to collect Social Security retirement benefits. Perhaps the medical problems you now fear may shorten your life will be cured in the near future!

Question 4. How Badly Will I Need the Money at Age 62?

Even though you will receive a smaller payment by taking early retirement, maybe you will really *need the money* (for food, rent, etc.). It's important to keep in mind that, even though your monthly payment will be reduced, postponing let's say $750 per month for say five years until age 67 adds up to $45,000. If you *"kick the bucket"* before 67, you are leaving the $45,000 you would have received on the table. In this scenario, money that could have made your life easier went uncollected. As things can sometimes turn out, the deprivation you endured may have been unnecessary!

Question 5. Do you Want Medicare at Age 65?

The 2016 *Medicare deductible* is $104 per month. Social Security will deduct this amount monthly if you are collecting monthly benefits. If you are delaying taking benefits and you want to start using Medicare at age 65, you will be responsible for paying this amount each month to Medicare. They will accept a payment by credit card but be sure to consider whether or not you want to add up to 29% in interest to your monthly Medicare payment.

Question 6. Savings, IRAs, Other Retirement Funds, Mattress Money, Friends and Relatives

Perhaps you have other funds available so that you can delay collecting SS benefits early. This is another option that you should add into the equation. Do you want to drain your bank account, sell your stock or empty your mutual fund account? Do you want to create potential future headaches by borrowing funds from friends or relatives? Don't be afraid to ask for advice from accountants, lawyers or people you trust. You want to make the best decision for your financial situation now and in the future!

Question 7. What is my Projected Expense Budget at Age 62?

I suggest that you prepare a projected age 62 budget. Write down all of your projected monthly expenses and leave some room for auto repairs or other emergencies. Don't forget day to day expenses as well. How will you cover these projected expenses? This will help you decide if you can wait until Full Retirement Age or even the maximum retirement age of 70 where waiting additional time before filing for benefits will no longer produce a larger monthly payment!

Don't Just Follow Others!

When other family members, friends and co-workers start to collect their Social Security may cloud your judgment. ***Don't let it!*** Everyone's situation is different and so is yours. Keep emotion out of your decision making. Just the facts and the numbers should help you decide your course of action and decisions regarding when you should start collecting your Social Security benefits.

Approximately half of all Americans claim their Social Security benefits at age 62. But keep in mind that if you wait until your full retirement age your monthly benefit payment can be up to approx. **31% higher.** If you can wait until age 70 to start collecting, your payment can jump up to approx. **75% higher** than the age 62 monthly benefit payment.

When is Break Even?

If you start taking SS monthly benefits at full retirement age rather than the early retirement age of 62, your break even age will be approx. around 83 years of age. From this point on, you will be receiving a larger monthly payment, again as we said above, **31%**

to 75% higher *for the rest of your life.* The above also applies if you wait until age 70 to start collecting monthly benefits.

Retire Early and Invest the Money?

Many people consider taking early retirement and investing the money as a possible way to *"beat the system."* But consider these facts:

[a] Postponing the start of receiving early retirement benefits at age 62 will increase your benefit checks by 7% to 8% per year until age 70. And this is guaranteed money adjusted annually for inflation by the U.S. Government!

[b] You know how little the banks are paying in savings account interest in year 2016. Even Money Market and Treasury Bills cannot match the guaranteed return described above!

[c] You know how volatile the stock market can be. *Do you really want to put your retirement money at risk?*

What About My Spouse?

Your Spouse cannot file for SS Spousal Benefits until you file for your SS retirement benefits. If you file for SS retirement benefits and your spouse files for spousal benefits before reaching her/his full retirement age, the spouse can lose the ability to switch to the highest possible benefit in the future.

If your spouse was employed and qualifies for his or her own SS retirement benefits at age 62, you should consider having your spouse wait until full retirement age [66/67] and then filing to collect Spousal Benefits under your account [50% of your monthly benefit amount] until age 70 and then filing for her own SS Retirement Benefits which should be a larger amount each month than the Spousal Benefits she was receiving under your account [naturally check these amounts with SS before making your final decisions].

"File and Suspend" is Now Suspended

Social Security used to allow a husband, for example, to file for benefits at Full Retirement Age and immediately suspend receiving monthly benefits. This allowed his wife to file for Spousal Benefits and receive 50% of what the husband should be receiving before he suspended the payments. Now the husband will wait until age 70 before resuming payments so that his benefit payments will be higher [remember the 7-8% per year increase rule] when he resumes them at age 70. The Social Security Administration **cancelled** "File and Suspend" as of April 2016.

How Much Will I Receive Monthly?

How much you receive monthly will be based on your earnings over your working years and the age you decide to file for SS monthly benefits. The average monthly benefit is about $1200 per month. It can be as high as around $3500 for high income earners who wait until age 70 to collect. It can be as low as $300 for those deciding to file at early retirement age. See the chart below which assumes a monthly benefit of $1000 at full retirement age.

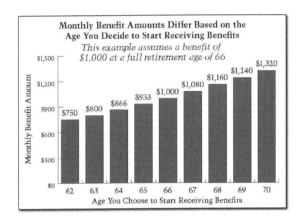

The SSA uses complicated formulas to calculate your Primary Insurance Amount. You can visit the Social Security website where benefit calculators can provide you with a more exact estimate of what your monthly benefits will be when you decide to take them.

What if I am Divorced?

If your marriage lasted a *minimum of 10 years* and you have not remarried, you should be able to claim SS benefits based on your former spouse's work history. You will only want to consider this if these benefits will be greater than the benefits you could receive based on your own work history. Remember, you will only be receiving 50% of your former spouse's monthly benefit and that's only if you wait until FRA.

If you start collecting at age 62 you will receive less. If the marriage ended more than two years ago, the good news is that you do not have to wait until your X files for monthly SS benefits as a current spouse must do. And your filing will have no effect on your X's benefits when he or she files. You will be entitled to receive 50% of your X's full retirement benefit, again at your FRA.

What if My "X" Passes Away?

If your previous spouse passes away, instead of collecting 50% spousal benefits, you will be entitled to receive 100% of the monthly amount that your former spouse was entitled to receive. Survivors benefits can start at age 60 (50 if you are legally disabled). But keep in mind that your monthly benefits will still be reduced if you claim them before your FRA. Please also be aware that divorced former spouses will not receive the SS lump-sum death benefit paid to surviving spouses or children (only $255.00 in year 2016) Remember, you can also switch between collecting your own SS benefits or spousal or survivor's benefits, taking whatever will yield you the most on a monthly basis.

What if I Remarry?

You may lose your spousal or survivors benefits based on your X's earning history but there are exceptions.

If you are over 60 years of age (over 50 if disabled), you can continue to claim survivor's benefits based on your X's earning history.

If your new marriage ends in divorce or your new spouse passes away, you may again become eligible for benefits under your first X's earning history no matter how long the new marriage lasted. If the new marriage lasted for a minimum of 10 years, then you will have the luxury of choosing which X's earning history will be more beneficial for you to claim benefits against.

Caring for X's Children Under 16 or Disabled

Even if your marriage didn't last 10 years or you have not reached retirement age and your X passes away, you may be eligible to claim benefits of up to 75% of your X's full retirement benefit as a surviving divorced parent caring for your X's natural or legally adopted child. Since this may get complicated I suggest you phone SSA toll free at **1-800-772-1213 for free advice** or visit the nearest SSA office.

Decisions for Widows and Widowers

When a spouse dies, the hope is that there is sufficient life insurance to cover funeral expenses and living expenses for a period of time. This could help you to strategize your Social Security benefits to your maximum benefit. If you worked and qualify for your own retirement benefits, you will have to choose between collecting survivor benefits and your own retirement benefits. You cannot collect both simultaneously but you can switch from one to the other to maximize your monthly income.

Widows and widowers can start receiving survivor benefits at age 60 but at about 70% less than they would receive at FRA.

A Strategy to Maximize Monthly Benefits

Let's say that a widow loses her husband who would have received *higher* SS monthly benefits at his FRA than she would at FRA. If she can afford to wait until her early retirement age of 62 to start collecting her own retirement benefits which let's say is $1100 per month (which will be around $1500 at FRA) she can continue to take these $1100 monthly checks to pay the bills and then, when she reaches her FRA of say 66, she can switch to start receiving her deceased husband's benefits as survivor benefits. If her husband's benefits would be $1900 per month, she will now receive an *extra $800* per month for the rest of her life.

Since these type of cases are more complicated than a person just filing for retirement benefits, and every case can be different for widows and widowers, I suggest that you visit a SS office in your area and sit down with a SS counselor and review all of your possible scenarios and make detailed notes.

Since money is involved and it may be monthly payments for the rest of your life which can translate into thousands of dollars gained or lost depending on the decisions you will make, I would also seek the advice of a professional accountant or SS attorney or at least seek the advice of knowledgeable friends, relatives or even a priest or social worker who can find you a knowledgeable advisor at little or no cost. Remember, you may live to age 95 or even older, so do everything possible to maximize your monthly benefit payments.

The Right to Appeal SSA Decisions

The good news is that you have the *right to appeal* any decision SSA makes regarding whether or not you are entitled to Social Security benefits. You can start by asking for a review of the initial decision. If the matter is not resolved, you have 60 days to request a hearing. You are entitled to bring an attorney or someone to assist you. If you cannot resolve the matter you can request a hearing before an Administrative Law Judge. Beyond that you can take your case to the *Federal District Court* which will usually require an attorney.

CHAPTER TWO

Social Security Disability Insurance [SSDI]

Any of us can become disabled at any time through accident or illness so it's nice to know that our government does offer us some protection so that we can keep eating. Here are some SDDI statistics from the SSA (2014).

The average age of a disabled person collecting SSDI is **53** with **men** representing **over 51 percent**. According to SSA, a study has shown that a 20-year-old

worker has a one-in-four chance of becoming disabled before reaching full retirement age.

The average monthly benefit was **$1,165.39** and the largest cause of disability was for diseases of the musculoskeletal system and connective tissue (31.2 percent). Disability benefits have been paid to over 10.2 million people. As of December 2014, payments to disabled beneficiaries totaled more than $11.4 billion dollars.

CBS' *60 Minutes* devoted several shows to expose widespread fraud on SSDI. In West Virginia and Mississippi, a small number of attorneys have succeeded in getting SSDI for large numbers of previously rejected applicants. *Less than half* of those who apply without the help of an attorney succeed in receiving benefits.

Who is Eligible for SSDI?

If you worked enough time (see 2 charts below), if your boss paid your FICA taxes, and if you have a medical or health condition that is expected to *last at least one year* or result in death, then you may qualify for SSDI benefits. The processing of your application for SSDI can take *3 to 5 months, possibly longer,* if your application is denied and you must file an appeal. As they say on the high seas during a storm, you may have to *"batten down the hatches"* to make sure you will be able to

keep paying the rent and eating during this tough period. If you are receiving benefits from any city or state programs, they may affect your application for SSDI benefits. Discuss this with a SSDI counselor or with a Disability Attorney if you are able to hire one.

To claim disability benefits, you must meet two different earnings tests:

[1] A recent work test based on your age at the time you became disabled (see below chart).

Rules for work needed for the recent work test	
If you become disabled...	Then, you generally need:
In or before the quarter you turn age 24	1.5 years of work during the three-year period ending with the quarter your disability began.
In the quarter after you turn age 24 but before the quarter you turn age 31	Work during half the time for the period beginning with the quarter after you turned 21 and ending with the quarter you became disabled. Example: If you become disabled in the quarter you turned age 27, then you would need three years of work out of the six-year period ending with the quarter you became disabled.
In the quarter you turn age 31 or later	Work during five years out of the 10-year period ending with the quarter your disability began.

[2] A duration of work test to show that you worked long enough under Social Security (see chart below).

Examples of work needed for the duration of work test	
If you become disabled...	Then, you generally need:
Before age 28	1.5 years of work
Age 30	2 years
Age 34	3 years
Age 38	4 years
Age 42	5 years
Age 44	5.5 years
Age 46	6 years
Age 48	6.5 years
Age 50	7 years
Age 52	7.5 years
Age 54	8 years
Age 56	8.5 years
Age 58	9 years
Age 60	9.5 years

Paperwork Required for Filing for SSDI Benefits

I recommend that you phone SSA or visit their website to see the latest list of the documents they require you to file in order to qualify for SSDI benefits. For some documents, such as birth certificates, SSA will require the originals so that is why I suggest you try to bring them to an SSA office personally instead of mailing them. In addition, make yourself backup copies of all documents before handing them in to SSA.

Information and Documents Required for SSDI

- SSA Application Forms and any forms or documents from medical professionals you have seen. SSA will help you with the forms, information and documents so do not delay. Bring whatever documents you can provide as quickly as possible in order to save time.

- Birth Certificate or Baptismal Certificate (SSA will want the original)

- Your Social Security number

- Names, addresses and phone numbers of all the medical professionals you have seen, including the dates of your visits

- Copies of all medical records you have in your possession, including copies of all laboratory tests and results

- A list of all medications you are taking, including dosages

- Your employment history including dates, names, addresses and phone numbers

- Your most recent W-2 Form or Federal Tax Returns if you had your own business

When dealing with the SSA it is important to keep detailed records of your interactions. **Keep a log** which lists the names of everyone you speak to, what was said, and include dates and times.

What Happens Next?

SSA will review your application forms, documents and information. If everything goes well, they will forward your case to the **Disability Determination Services Office** in your state for further processing.

SSA uses a 5 step procedure to help them decide if you meet their qualifications for being disabled.

(a) Are you **now working** full-time or part-time?

(b) Is your medical condition considered *"severe"?*

(c) Do your impairments meet SSA's *List of Conditions* which they consider severe enough to prevent a person from engaging in gainful employment and activities?

(d) Are you currently able to perform the work you did previously?

(e) Are you able to perform any type of work?

Please note that there are special rules for the blind. Contact SSA for more information.

If You Are Approved

If SSA **approves** your application, you will receive a letter informing you of the amount of your monthly benefit and when payments will begin. If you are **denied**, the letter will tell you why and explain the process of filing an appeal.

Getting a Disability Attorney to Help You

If you feel that your disability case is complicated or have reservations about filing a claim with SSA, I suggest that you talk to a disability attorney who offers a free consultation. My research indicates that filing for disability and getting rejected and then hiring a disability attorney to do an appeal for you takes a lot more time than if you have an attorney help you file in the first place. In addition, I suggest that you look for a disability attorney who has successful SSA experience with clients with your type of injury, medical condition or disability. Please consider this suggestion carefully.

Hiring A Disability Attorney

There are plenty of disability attorneys advertising on the Internet, on TV and in the newspapers. You can also call your local Bar Association to ask for a list of disability lawyers. Speak to several and ask for references. Don't be shy. Ask questions. Does the attorney have the time to give you the attention you are now seeking? Will the attorney return your phone calls promptly? Will the attorney file your case or appeal quickly? You don't want delays because your attorney is busy with too many other clients.

Hire the attorney or law firm that you feel most comfortable with. If you have friends or relatives receiving SSDI, consider asking them to recommend an attorney to you.

Check out the website www.nolo.com. You will find disability attorneys listed by state. NOLO has been assisting consumers and businesses with legal information for the last 40 years.

Disability Attorney Fees

The good news is that you can hire a *contingency fee* disability attorney who will be paid only out of your past-due benefits or *"back pay."* SSA limits the fee disability attorneys can charge you to *25% of your past-due benefits up to a maximum of $6,000.* In addition, SSA deducts the entire lawyer's fee from your first disability check before the agency sends you the balance you are due.

Beware of Disability Attorney Expenses

Most disability attorneys will want you to pay their out-of-pocket expenses separately from their fees. They may have to request work records, medical and other documents on your behalf and they may have to arrange for you to be examined by other doctors to help you win your case.

- SSA permits an attorney to ask you for money in advance to cover expenses as long as the attorney holds the money in a bank trust account until needed.

- You can choose to look for an attorney who will advance expenses for clients. If the attorney asks you to sign an agreement stating that you will be responsible for expenses even if your case is unsuccessful, I suggest that you negotiate a cap *(maximum amount)* such as $250.00 to protect yourself from an unscrupulous attorney who may pad the bill.

Appealing SSDI Decisions

If you are denied SSDI benefits, you have the right to appeal. There are basically 4 stages of appeal for a disability claim for which I recommend that you seek the advice of a disability attorney.

- Reconsideration

- Administrative Hearing

- Appeals Council Review

- Taking your case to Federal District Court

You have 60 days to file a "Request for Reconsideration." If you again receive a denial of your claim, you have another 60 days to file for an Administrative Hearing before an Administrative Law Judge.

How About Benefits for My Family?

Based on your work history, some members of your family may qualify for SSDI benefits. They include:

- Your spouse, if she or he is age 62 (early retirement age) or older

- Your spouse at any age, if she or he is caring for a child. The child must be younger than 18 (or younger than 19 if still in school).

- Your child *(unmarried)*, age below 18, or older if she or he has a disability that started before age 22.

- A divorced spouse, if she or he was married to you for at least 10 years, is at least 62 years of age and not now married.

Medicare Health Coverage

If you are under age 65, you can get Medicare coverage automatically after you have received disability benefits *for two years.*

ABLE and the ABLE Act

On December 19, 2014 President Obama signed the Tax Extenders Package making the ABLE Act the law of the land. ABLE Accounts are tax-advantaged savings accounts for individuals with significant disabilities with an age onset of disability before turning age 26 years of age. It allows individuals, family and friends to put away up to $14,000 per year in a tax-advantaged savings account for the eligible disabled person without interfering with other city, state or federal benefits the disabled person may be eligible for. Most states participate in ABLE Act programs.

Visit the website www.ablenrc.org for additional information and a list of all participating states or do a Google search for ABLE Act or ABLE programs in your state. Ask someone at your local library for assistance if you do not have a computer with internet access.

Going Back to Work

The good news is that SSA has special rules called work incentives which allow you to test your ability to resume work while still receiving disability benefits. You can also get help with education, rehabilitation and the training you may need to resume work. Talk to your SSA counselor.

Work-at-Home Jobs

SSDI allows disabled persons to earn $1000 per month [$1640 if blind] without a reduction in benefits. **NTI,** a nonprofit organization, will help disabled Americans find legitimate online work-from-home jobs, at no cost, in customer service, technical support, telephone sales and other types of work which can be done from home using a computer and/or telephone. They can also help you get training while at home. You can phone them at **866-501-8387** or visit their website at www.ntiathome.org. For additional information about NTI's services visit www.mytickettoworkathome.org.

CHAPTER THREE

Some Important Info About Social Security

Again, while trying to keep this publication as short as possible in this new world of 140 character messages and even shorter text messages, there is some information that I believe may be too important for me to exclude. I will explain this information as succinctly as possible.

Same-Sex Married Couples

On June 26, 2015, the U.S. Supreme Court's decision [Obergefell v. Hodges] granted marriage equality to all couples regardless of gender or sexual orientation. Same-Sex couples and surviving spouses who were previously denied should reapply for benefits. The same rules for heterosexual married couples should now apply to same-sex married couples! Please contact SSA with any questions.

Social Security and Working Overseas

Since the USA has SS agreements with over 25 countries around the world, if you and your employer are both paying FICA taxes, your SS benefits should remain the same. SSA maintains an "Office of International Operations" which you can contact with any questions you may have. Their website is www.ssa.gov/foreign/index.html.

Criminal Convictions, Probation or Parole

You will not be eligible to receive Social Security Disability Insurance Benefits or Social Security Benefits if you are incarcerated, have an outstanding arrest warrant or have violated your conditions of Probation or Parole imposed under federal or state law. You are required to report any of the above situations to SSA immediately. The good news is that family members who are eligible for benefits can usually continue to receive them.

Create Your Own "My Social Security" Online Account

If you are over 18 years of age, have a Social Security number, a valid e-mail address, and have a U.S. mailing address, you can create your own personal account for your own use only on the SSA website. Keep in mind that giving any false information to SSA is a federal crime and that you are prohibited from creating an account for another person even if you have permission from

SOME IMPORTANT INFO ABOUT SOCIAL SECURITY

that person. If you are trying to help a disabled person, phone SSA for instructions.

When creating an online account, you will be asked to set up a user name and password. The password must be 8 characters' minimum and must contain at least one uppercase letter (A-Z), at least one lowercase letter (a-z), at least one number (0-9), at least one symbol (?@#$%^&*), and begin with a letter or number.

You will be able to monitor your earnings, benefit payments and all the information that SSA has about you. You will also be able to set up direct deposit where your monthly benefit payments will be deposited each month by SSA like clockwork. For direct deposit you must supply your bank's routing code

and account number to SSA. There are many advantages to choosing direct deposit. You can still request that SSA mail you a check each month but if it gets lost or stolen, you will have to go through the hassle of getting it replaced. You will be much better off with direct deposit.

It is important that you set up your "My Social Security" account before a scammer sets one up in your name with the money going to one of their bank accounts. This has been happening a lot. An increase in the data breaches of computers belonging to retail stores and other businesses has given the scammers access to millions of social security numbers along with other personal information which has enabled them to impersonate senior citizens!

When setting up your own "My Social Security" account, check off yes to **"add extra security"** on the online form. A new security code will be texted to your cell phone each time you attempt to log on which will help protect you from the scammers logging onto your account and having the direct deposit changed to one of their bank accounts! They will ask you for the last 8 digits of your Visa, MasterCard or Discover Card or information from your W2 tax form. Then they will mail you an upgrade letter that will arrive within 10 days. You will need this letter to complete the security upgrade process.

Benefit or No Benefit SSA Verification Letters

If you need a legal document to prove that you are receiving SS benefits, SSI, Disability or Medicare, or conversely that you are **NOT** receiving the above benefits; or to prove that you applied and were turned down, you can apply to SSA for a Verification Letter. You can use your "My Social Security" online account to request the Verification Letter, or you can phone SSA or visit one of their offices.

If You Need Additional Information About SS

The good news is that information on Social Security is not difficult to find but make sure that the information you obtain is up-to-date. For instance, many books on SS claim to have been updated for 2016 but still do not advise you that "File and Suspend" was cancelled by SSA in April 2016. Be sure to check the publication date of the information you are reading. Verify information that relates to your situation directly with SSA.

Sources of Additional Information on SS:

- **The Social Security Administration Website** (www.ssa.gov) free and provides the latest and most up-to-date information. Many seniors are not comfortable using the internet or have problems navigating, which may

- be upsetting! If this describes you, don't despair. You are not alone! If possible, try to find some Internet "Whiz-Kid" to help you. Please keep in mind that SSA has offices all over the country and hopefully there is one near you. **Phone SSA at 1-800-772-1213** for the address of the office closest to you and to set up an appointment to visit.

- **AARP**, Inc., formerly the American Association of Retired Persons, is a United States-based membership and interest group, founded in 1958 by Ethel Percy Andrus, Ph.D., a retired educator from California. If you are comfortable using the Internet, their website has a ton of information for you to read on SS. Visit www.arpp.org/work/social-security.

- **www.amazon.com/books** has many books on SS on their website but some are of the 200-300-page variety so check their book descriptions carefully. There are often sample pages available for you to read.

CHAPTER FOUR

Identity Theft and Protecting Your SS Number!

Identity Theft is still a big problem in the USA and worldwide. A recent study released by Javelin Strategy & Research, found that $16 billion was stolen from 12.7 million U.S. consumers in 2014. There was a new identity fraud victim every two seconds in 2014. Here's a breakdown of the types of identity theft fraud:

- Govt. documents or benefits fraud 38.7%
- Credit card fraud 17.4%
- Phone or utilities fraud 12.5%
- Bank fraud 8.2%
- Attempted identity theft 4.8%
- Employment-related fraud 4.8%
- Loan fraud 4.4%
- Other identity theft 21.8%

As you can see by the above numbers, Government documents and benefit fraud top the identity theft list so you must take precautions to protect your Social Security number and date of birth.

You may be thinking right now, I walk into the drug store and the first thing they ask me for is my date of birth. When I show them my Medicare Card, it shows my SS number as my Medicare number. And when I go into a doctor's office or hospital, they give me paperwork requiring my SS number and date of birth. I have heard of a number of cases where identity thieves pay clerks in doctors' offices and hospitals to copy your records and sell it to them. Once they have your name, address, date of birth, and SS number, they can try to steal your identity, steal your income tax refund, open accounts in your name and may even try to sell your home out from under you! I don't want to scare or depress you but I do want to help protect you.

Unfortunately, our open society is making life easy for the identity theft thieves. Our system is broken and we must all speak out loudly to try to correct it.

Some Ideas to Protect Yourself

Try to avoid giving out your SS number and date of birth. I generally leave the forms blank when I am asked for that information. And if the information is demanded, I ask how my information will be protected!

Never give out your SS number to a voice on the phone. The Social Security Administration will never ask you for this information on the phone and they will never phone you for personal information unless you are working with a particular case worker who you will know by name and phone number. When in doubt, get a caller's name and phone number and call SSA at 1-800-772-1213 to verify that the person calling works for SSA.

Protect Your Bank Checking Account

Whenever you pay a bill by mailing a personal check from your checking account, you may be giving identity thieves the information they need to clean out your checking account.

Even mailing a check to pay Walmart or Sears may put you in jeopardy. The check may be stolen in the mail or a crooked employee may copy your checking account number and routing code. Anyone can purchase check software on the Internet that is designed to print checks with any routing code and any account number to draft any checking account. The banks check very few signatures these days. Everything is electronic and digital. The whole system makes life easy for the identity thieves and really needs to be changed for the protection of the general public!

Here's what I recommend to protect yourself. It's easy to get a free personal checking account in most cities. Some banks just want you to keep a $100 balance such as **TD bank in New York**. Even **Discover,** the credit card company now offers a *free* checking account.

I suggest that you keep secret the bank account that you use to have SSA make direct deposits of your SS benefits to. Set up a separate checking account to pay your bills and just transfer enough money to cover the checks you write. Keep your nest egg money in the "secret" checking account or in a Savings Account that you never use to transact business so that the account number remains a secret so to speak. Do the same with your Credit Card. Use a low limit credit card for Internet purchases. Use any high limit credit cards with extreme care. Never give out the high limit credit card account number on the Internet or the phone.

Nothing is 100% as even your own bank may have a crooked employee. But if you take precautions, the banks and credit card companies will also protect you from fraud to a limited extent!

Seniors Are Being Targeted

Since many of my readers are or will be seniors over the age of sixty I would like to do whatever I can to provide good advice which can protect them.

Unfortunately, there are many scammers out there attempting to take advantage of senior citizens. They are well aware that some seniors may be experiencing the early stages of Alzheimer's disease, dementia or other age-related memory problems, or other ailments which may make them more vulnerable to scammers.

There are mailing list providers on the Internet who will rent the names of seniors to anyone willing to pay. Scammers may be able to select individuals from a mailing list by age, if they use a credit card, geographic location and other personal details that the mailing list houses purchase from credit bureaus and data mining companies. Unfortunately, scammers are using digital technology to take advantage of seniors.

Protect Your Relatives, Friends and Yourself!

Unfortunately, when a senior gets scammed, the scammers will try to take advantage of them over and over again and they will sell their names to other scammers. Many seniors are too embarrassed to tell their family and friends that they have been cheated. Tragically some have even committed suicide after being cleaned out by the scammers. Try your best to look for any telltale signs of financial problems from your senior relatives and friends. Perhaps they will let you monitor their bank, credit card statements and Credit Bureau reports to see if there has been suspicious financial activity. Look over your monthly statements carefully each month as well.

Free Credit Bureau Reports

Federal law allows you to obtain a free copy of your Credit Bureau Report once per year from each of the 3 major Credit Bureaus: Equifax, Transunion and Experian. There is really only one legitimate website the government set up to accomplish this which is https://www.annualcreditreport.com/ Beware of the many websites with very similar names which will ask you for money or even attempt to sign you up for monthly or annual subscriptions.

I suggest that you get a **Free Credit Bureau Report** from one of the bureaus every two or 3 months. Then get a free report from one of the other two, and so on. Be prepared for each Credit Bureau to ask you all kinds of "crazy" questions to verify your identity. They may ask you which of several cars you owned in the past and which of several addresses you lived at in the past and similar type questions. Some of these questions may date back 20 or 30 years so be prepared to respond to the best of your ability.

Free Credit Score

The above mentioned Credit Bureaus will give you free copies of your credit bureau reports but they will want to charge you for your **Credit Score**. You can obtain a **FREE** copy of your Credit Score from www.creditkarma.com. As of this writing, they will not ask you for any money. Your Credit Score is what banks and lenders use to determine your credit worthiness. In addition, you can also check out www.creditsesame.com. They are similar to Credit Karma but they also offer Free Credit Monitoring for fraud protection. Be aware that companies offering free credit monitoring, or free anything, may sell your personal information to Data Marketing Companies.

CHAPTER FIVE

Social Security Scams to Watch Out For

Not only are seniors targeted for all kinds of scams (especially financial scams), but it's too easy for scammers to purchase a list of 66-year old's with the general knowledge that most of them are receiving SS retirement or SS spousal benefits.

Scam Prevention Rules of the Road

- Never give personal information to an incoming phone caller unless you are 100% sure who the caller is. Get the caller's name and phone number and call them back after verifying that the phone number is the main phone number of the organization or business. Scammers can fake the Caller ID so that the call looks like it's coming from SSA or a legitimate organization. Don't fall for it.

- Callers often can sound so convincing on the phone that the recipient of the phone call lets his or her guard down. Again, don't fall for it. It's called "Social Engineering."

- Callers often claim that they need sensitive information to verify who you are. Try to avoid giving out complete information. Only give the last 4 digits of your social security number or credit card or only the month of your birthday.

- Scammers will duplicate the website of SSA, your bank, your credit card company, etc. and try to scam you on your computer. Log out and log into the legitimate URL [web address] of the agency or business.

- Scammers will copy the letterhead of SSA, your bank, credit card company, department store, etc. and send a mailing to you asking you to phone them. Log onto google or call

- directory assistance and verify that the phone number is for real and not a scammer.

- Beware of strangers knocking on your door, sometimes wearing a construction worker helmet and construction clothing, claiming that you have a water leak or they want to read your meter. They may offer to give you a free estimate on cleaning your chimney or repairing your roof.

- Beware of well-dressed strangers claiming to be from Social Security or the IRS. They may even have phony ID. These agencies will not send people to your home unannounced. They will contact you by mail about any problems beforehand.

- Get their business card and tell anyone appearing at your door that they must wait outside until you can verify who they are. Double lock the door and get on the phone and attempt to verify whoever it is. If you feel in danger, phone the police. They will not mind sending a car to verify the people at your door.

- Am I trying to make you paranoid? The answer is YES! I would rather have you waste a little of your time than lose your life savings or even your life!

The COLA Scam

In most years, your SS benefits will increase by a small percentage once per year to keep up with inflation. This is called the **"Cost-of-living-adjustment".** The increase is automatic and will be added to your check or direct deposit account. You do not have to do anything. Unfortunately, there was no COLA in 2016 because lower energy prices kept inflation down last year.

The scammers may try to take advantage of this situation by phoning, texting, emailing or mailing you a letter claiming that in order for you to get the COLA for 2016, you must fill out a form or supply certain information. Those who supply this information may have their SS benefits or identities stolen. Again, don't fall for it!

The Data-Breach Scam

You may get a phone call, text, email or letter telling you that SSA's computers have been broken into and that your account may have been hacked. They claim that they are in the process restoring everything but they need you to verify the information that they have on file. They will proceed to give you false information such as a bogus bank account number.

They expect you to say "that's not my account number". They will tell you that your benefit money is scheduled to go into that account. Now, they have you so confused and upset that you will beg them to allow you to give them your correct bank account number. Now you get the idea of how social engineering works. The caller makes you believe that they are from the SSA and are trying to help you. Once you believe it, you can be in big trouble.

Prevention is very simple. Whenever you get any type of contact from someone claiming to be from the SSA, you need to call the legitimate phone number of **SSA at 1-800-772-1213** and ask them if there is any problem with your account.

Digital Chip Social Security Card Scam

If you use credit cards, you are probably aware of the new credit cards being issued with a chip to replace the older cards with just the magnetic stripe. The new chip is called EMV technology which stands for Euro Pay MasterCard and Visa [EMV] which have been used in Europe for years.

The new credit cards contain a very small computer chip that's extremely difficult to counterfeit. Stores and businesses accepting credit cards were supposed to upgrade their credit card machines by October 1, 2015 to accept the new chip cards which slide into a slot in the new credit card terminals.

If the stores do not upgrade their equipment and use the magnetic stripe that the new cards still have, the stores will be responsible if the card is stolen or fraudulent and the banks and credit card companies will not reimburse the merchants for their financial loss in the transaction.

Unfortunately, the Social Security scam artists have jumped on this and are calling seniors claiming that they are calling from the SSA claiming that records show that you did not upgrade to the new Social Security Chip Cards and that your benefits will be suspended until you do so. Then they offer to **"overnight"** a new SS chip card to you but they must verify your identity before they can send it. They will ask for your personal information. If you give it to them, they can steal your SS benefits and/or steal your identity, which may be even worse.

Social Security cards are never swiped in card readers and there are no Social Security cards containing chips. Don't fall for any phone calls, text messages, emails or letters, telling you otherwise. Always **phone SSA at 1-800-772-1213 to verify any contacts** you receive claiming to be from SSA.

Beware of Other SS Scams and Fraud

The scammers are always coming up with new schemes to get your money so always be on guard. Be sure to discuss these scams with your relatives and friends and be sure to keep your eye on anyone who may be especially vulnerable!

CHAPTER SIX

The Future of Social Security and Medicare

Happy 81th Anniversary!

Social Security was signed into law on August 14, 1935 by President Franklin Delano Roosevelt. On August 14, 2016, SS enjoyed its 81th Anniversary. Approximately 10,000 Americans turn 65 each day. This number of new retirees will continue for the next 15 years. The over 85 group is the fastest growing portion of our population followed by the growing over 100 years of age super seniors group! It costs an average of $87,000 per year to live in a nursing home in 2016. Our aging population presents many financial challenges in the years ahead.

Social Security Trust Funds may be Depleted in 2034

Each year the trustees of the Social Security and Medicare trust funds report on the current and projected financial status of the two programs each year. Following is a *brief summary* of their **2016 Annual Report.**

The Social Security Program provides workers and their families with retirement, disability and survivor's insurance benefits. Over the program's 81-year history, it has collected roughly $19.0 trillion and paid out $16.1 trillion, leaving asset reserves of more than $2.8 trillion at the end of 2015 in its two trust funds. The trustees project that the combined two Social Security trust funds will be depleted in 2034.

The above summary does not conclude that retirees will not receive benefit checks in 2034. It is possible that SSA's *"old Age Fund"* will only be able to pay out approximately 80% of promised benefits. So if

you are looking forward to $1500 per month, you may only be getting $1200 per month in the year 2034 if nothing is done to correct the situation.

The SSDI disability fund is in worse shape and could be depleted by year 2023 which means that it may only be able to pay approximately 90% of promised disability benefits.

Some Suggested Social Security Fixes

If we want to fix Social Security and make it solvent for the next 50 years, here are some of the current popular suggestions:

- Raise the SS payroll tax from 12.4% to 15% on the first $118,500 of taxable income.

- Forget the $118,500 tax limit and tax total income regardless of the amount earned per year.

- Create a Means Test. Too many people are collecting SS that are wealthy and really do not need the money.

- Raise Retirement Age (which has already happened to some extent).

- Cut SS benefits. Our politicians on both sides of the aisle are afraid of this one!

- Privatize. Allow workers to put their retirement money in the stock market to grow or go bust!

These are just a few of many ideas people and politicians have about fixing SS and hopefully some intelligent compromises will prevail in the years ahead. Write and phone your Senators and Congressman and let them know where you stand on fixing Social Security and Medicare!

Part of Medicare May Be in Trouble in Year 2028

Many seniors who depend on Medicare will be reading this book. Here is brief but important rundown on what the near future of Medicare currently looks like.

The Medicare Program consists of two separate trust funds, the Hospital Insurance Trust Fund [HI] and the Supplementary Medical Insurance Trust Fund [SMI]. HI is called Medicare Part A and helps pay for hospital, home health services following hospital stays, and skilled nursing facility and hospice care for the aged and disabled. SMI consists of Medicare Part B and Part D. Part B helps pay for physician, outpatient hospital, home health and other services for the aged and disabled who have voluntarily - enrolled. Part D provides subsidized access to drug insurance coverage on a voluntary basis for beneficiaries and premium and cost-sharing subsidies for low-income enrollees.

The Trustees project that HI **[Medicare Part A]** will be **depleted in 2028**, two years earlier than projected in last year's 2015 report and will only be able to pay out 87% of expected benefits in 2028.

Medicare [SMI] **Part B and Part D** is funded by a combination of premium payments and money from the general federal revenue. The good news is that **both will be financed in-full indefinitely**, but only because the current law (which could be changed in the future) requires automatic financing of both programs.

"Social Security and Medicare Remain Secure in the Medium-Term" ...

So said our 2016 Treasury Secretary Jacob Lew. "But reform will be needed," he added, "and Congress should not wait until the eleventh hour to address the fiscal challenges given that they represent the cornerstone of economic security for seniors in our country."

I hope You Liked This Book…

In this book I tried to unlock the many mysteries of Social Security in a brief and easy to understand format. I would appreciate your input. Please consider writing **a review** for this book **on Amazon.com**. Log onto Amazon's website and search **"Social Security Quick and Easy."** Click on *product detail page,* then click *customer reviews* and finally click *write a review*. After you write the review, click *submit!*

Please E-mail Me …

to receive updates to this book and to learn about my new books as they are published. Please send your email to

ron7mail@gmail.com

and I will add you to my special email list. Please also let me know how you liked this book and what you would like to see in *future updated editions.*

Thank you for purchasing and reading my book. I sincerely hope that it helped you, your family and friends!

Ron Stewart

Addendum

Age To Receive Full Social Security Benefits
(Called "full retirement age" or "normal retirement age.")

Year of Birth *	Full Retirement Age
1937 or earlier	65
1938	65 and 2 months
1939	65 and 4 months
1940	65 and 6 months
1941	65 and 8 months
1942	65 and 10 months
1943--1954	66
1955	66 and 2 months
1956	66 and 4 months
1957	66 and 6 months
1958	66 and 8 months
1959	66 and 10 months
1960 and later	67

Made in the USA
San Bernardino, CA
15 October 2017